# KINGFISHER KNOWLEDGE

# STARS & PLANETS

▼ The space shuttle *Discovery* leaves the launchpad at the Kennedy Space Center, Florida, USA, in April 1990. This mission carried the *Hubble Space Telescope* into orbit around the Earth. *Hubble* looks into deep space, revealing far distant galaxies as well as the wonders of our own galaxy, the Milky Way.

KINGFISHER KNOWLEDGE

# STARS & PLANETS

## Carole Stott

Foreword by
**Sir Patrick Moore**

KINGFISHER

Editor: Vicky Weber
Senior designer: Peter Clayman
Picture researcher: Rachael Swann
Senior production controller: Lindsey Scott
DTP manager: Nicky Studdart
Artwork archivist: Wendy Allison
Indexer and proofreader: Sheila Clewley

KINGFISHER
Kingfisher Publications Plc, New Penderel House,
283–288 High Holborn, London WC1V 7HZ
www.kingfisherpub.com

First published by Kingfisher Publications Plc 2005
First published in paperback 2007
10 9 8 7 6 5 4 3 2 1
1TR/1206/TWP/MA(MA)/130ENSOMA/F

ISBN: 978 0 7534 1200 8

**GO FURTHER...**
**INFORMATION PANEL KEY:**

 websites and
further reading

 career paths

 places to visit

**NOTE TO READERS**
The website addresses listed in this book are correct
at the time of going to print. However, due to the
ever-changing nature of the internet, website addresses
and content can change. Websites can contain links
that are unsuitable for children. The publisher cannot
be held responsible for changes in website addresses or
content, or for information obtained through third-party
websites. We strongly advise that internet searches
should be supervised by an adult.

# Contents

▼ This view of the rust-coloured landscape of Mars was taken by the *Spirit* rover, which landed on the planet in January 2004. *Spirit's* aim was to study the martian rocks and soil, and search for evidence that liquid water was on Mars in the past.

# Foreword

Astronomy is one of the best of all hobbies. If you make up your mind to take a real interest in it, it can absorb as much – or as little – of your time and energy as you wish. Moreover, it is just about the only science in which amateurs can make useful contributions, and in which professional workers are glad of amateur help. How does a newcomer start out? Obviously, by looking up at the sky, reading, and becoming familiar with basic facts. Carole Stott is ideally qualified to provide the right book to excite your interest and she does just this in *KFK Stars & Planets* in a way that is absorbing and informative.

The book begins by introducing the basic structure of the Universe, and then goes on to discuss its birth and development, from the Big Bang, over 13 billion years ago, up to the present time. It explains how stars are born, how they go through their lives, and how they die – some of them quietly, others violently. We find out how much we can learn from the Sun, to which we owe our very existence and which is the ruler of the Solar System, our own particular part of the Universe. The focus then turns to our nearest neighbours, the Moon and planets – men have been to the Moon, and space probes have made close studies of the eight main planets. All these developments are discussed, and *KFK Stars & Planets* gives the very latest information.

Spacecraft also enter the picture, as do the great telescopes which make it possible for us to peer out into the far reaches of the Universe and see star systems so remote that their light has taken thousands, millions or even billions of years to reach us. It is quite amazing how much we have found out in the last few decades. Indeed, things are not quite what we believed them to be only a few years ago – there are no canal-building Martians and no oceans on Venus. However, the excitement is as great as ever, and all of us can share in it.

Reading this book will really broaden your knowledge of the stars and planets. Look at the night sky and find some of the stars and constellations featured in the book, such as Orion, Sirius and the Great Bear; buy or borrow a pair of binoculars to show you the craters of the Moon, the glorious star fields of the Milky Way and the rich star clusters such as Orion's Belt. Why not then think about joining your local astronomical society? You will not regret it. Who knows? One day you may yourself discover an exploding star, or a brilliant comet!

I wish I had had this much information when I started out, many years ago. Instead, let me wish you much pleasure as you read this fascinating and eye-opening book from one of the leading astronomical authors.

*Patrick Moore*

Sir Patrick Moore has written numerous books on astronomy. Since 1957, he has presented every one of the BBC's *The Sky at Night* programmes, a fact which has earned him a place in the *Guinness Book of Records* as the longest-serving television presenter. In 2001, Sir Patrick received a knighthood from the Queen.

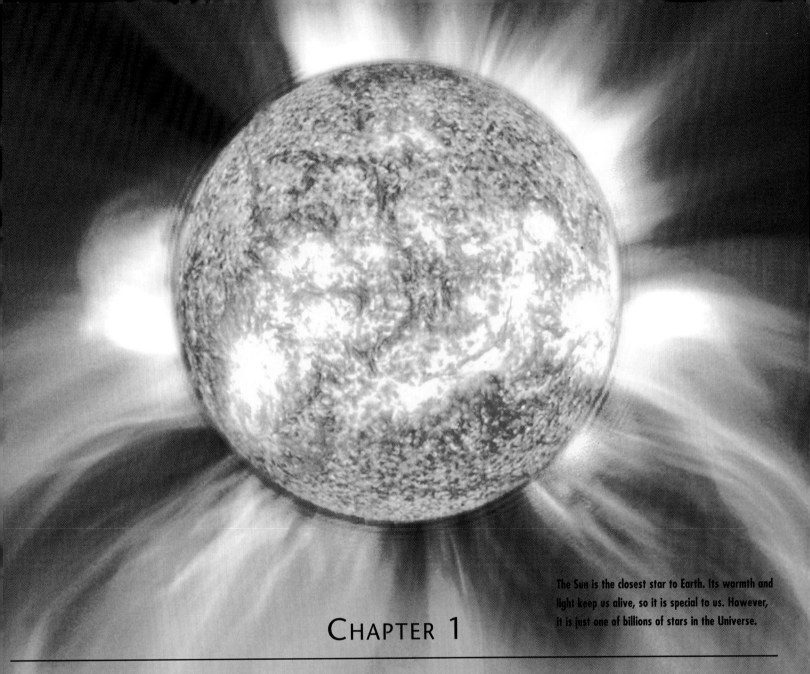

The Sun is the closest star to Earth. Its warmth and light keep us alive, so it is special to us. However, it is just one of billions of stars in the Universe.

CHAPTER 1

# A Universe of stars

Stars surround planet Earth. At night, hundreds of them shine as fixed dots of light in a cloudless sky. In the daytime, just one, the brilliant orange-yellow Sun, is on show. It is so close that it outshines all the other stars in the sky. Many of the stars are like our Sun – they shine brightly and steadily. Others are bigger or smaller, brighter or dimmer, hotter or cooler. Some spin around many times every second and some explode into space. All of the stars we see belong to our home galaxy – the Milky Way – a huge collection of stars. Billions more galaxies are scattered across the vast distances of space. There are more stars than anything else in the Universe – that seemingly endless stretch of space and everything that exists within it.

# Vast Universe

**W**hichever way we look out from Earth and however far we peer into space, we see galaxies. There are billions of them – each one an immense group of stars, gas and dust. They are scattered throughout space, with huge, virtually empty distances separating neighbours. These galaxies are like remote islands in our vast Universe.

### Islands in space

Galaxies are huge and each consists of billions of stars. Yet galaxies are not the biggest structures in the Universe. They are grouped into clusters, which are loosely strung together into superclusters – the biggest structures of all. These are linked across space. Between each supercluster, cluster and galaxy are enormous regions of empty space.

◄ Powerful telescopes such as this one called *Keck*, based in Hawaii, let us see deep into the Universe.

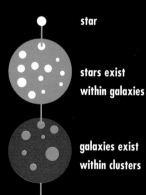

star

stars exist within galaxies

galaxies exist within clusters

clusters exist within superclusters

▲ The further we look into space, the more galaxies we see. Here, we are gazing deeper than ever before. Our view is part of a photograph taken by the *Hubble Space Telescope* that has revealed nearly 10,000 galaxies of different ages, sizes, shapes and colours. The most distant are about 12 billion light years away.

## Galaxy shapes

The stars in a galaxy stay together because of the pulling force called gravity. Each star follows its own orbit, or path, around the galaxy's centre. Together, the stars give a galaxy its shape – there are four basic patterns. Elliptical galaxies are ball-shaped. Spiral galaxies are pancake-shaped with a bulging centre and two or more arms of stars spiralling outwards. Barred spirals have a central bar of stars, and arms that wind out from either end. Some galaxies have no particular shape – these are the irregulars.

## Size of the Universe

Distances across the Universe, or even across a galaxy, are so enormous that the units of measurement used on Earth, such as the kilometre, are inadequate. Instead, measurements across the Universe have their own unit, called the light year. One light year is 9.46 trillion (million million) km – the distance that light travels in a year. That works out at 299,792km/sec. This is an incredible speed – in fact, light travels more swiftly than anything else in the Universe. The Whirlpool Galaxy is about 25 million light years away. That is much easier than saying it lies at a distance of 236,500,000,000,000,000,000km!

▲ The elliptical galaxy, M87, is one of the brightest galaxies. It belongs to the Virgo cluster, which consists of over 2,000 galaxies in a region 10 million light years wide.

▲ The barred-spiral galaxy, NGC 1300, has an arm of stars spinning away from each end of its central bar. It measures 85,000 light years from one side to the other.

▲ The Whirlpool Galaxy is a spiral galaxy. Young, bright stars make its arms stand out. There are stars in between as well, but they are outshone by the brilliance of the arms.

▲ The irregular galaxy, NGC 7673, is about 150 million light years from Earth. Like other irregulars it is rich in gas and dust and is always busy producing new stars.

# Bang!

The Universe has existed for over 13 billion years. Astronomers have worked out that it all started in an explosion called the Big Bang. This was the start of everything – the start of time, of space and of all there is in the Universe. Way back then, the Universe looked nothing like it does now. It was unbelievably small, unbearably hot and consisted of tiny bits of energy. From the instant of creation, the Universe has been changing into the one we know today.

8.3 light minutes from Earth

▲ We see the Sun as it was eight minutes and 19 seconds ago. It is 8.3 light minutes from Earth – 149.6 million km.

### Looking back in time

Incredibly, we can look back in time and see the Universe long ago. We can do this thanks to light – the fastest traveller in the Universe. Switch on a lamp and its light seems to reach your eyes instantly. Turn it off and the light is gone. If the Sun were turned off, it would be over eight minutes before we would notice. That is how long it takes for sunlight to reach Earth. The light from distant stars and galaxies takes much longer to reach us. When we look at them, we see them as they were when light left them billions of years ago. Some of the most distant galaxies ever found are about 12 billion light years away. This means it has taken some 12 billion years for their light to reach us, so we see these galaxies as they were when the Universe was very young.

◀ Belgian astronomer Georges Lemaître (1894–1966) was the first person to work out that the Universe is expanding (getting bigger) as a result of a huge explosion. He suggested that the Universe started as an extremely dense (tightly packed) ball of material and then exploded.

8.6 light years from Earth

2.4 million light years from Earth

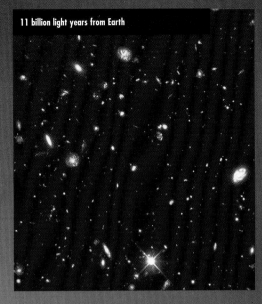

11 billion light years from Earth

▲ The brightest star in Earth's night sky is Sirius (centre top) in the constellation Canis Major. Its light takes 8.6 years to reach us.

▲ The spiral-shaped Andromeda Galaxy measures roughly 150,000 light years from side to side (1.4 billion billion km).

▲ We are looking at these galaxies just two billion years after the Big Bang, at a time when many giant galaxies were forming.

## Back to the beginning

At the very start, the Universe was super-hot and ultra-dense; it has been cooling and getting bigger ever since. Even before the first trillionth of a second was over, the Universe had ballooned in size. In less than a second, it had cooled to 10 billion °C and its energy particles became tiny bits of matter – the building blocks of all the material in today's Universe. By the end of three minutes, the first elements – hydrogen and helium – had formed. By then, around three quarters of the Universe was hydrogen and almost all the rest was helium. The Universe stayed pretty much like this for the next 250,000 years, although it continued to cool and grow bigger. All this time, the Universe was opaque, which means that it was sort of foggy and light could not pass through it. So, when we look back at far distant stars and galaxies, we can only go back to about 300,000 years after the Big Bang – telescopes cannot show us what it was like before that time.

▼ The timeline below, which continues on pages 12 and 13, shows the evolution of the Universe from the Big Bang right up to today. The scale below the blue line shows how much time has passed since the Big Bang. The captions above the blue line tell you what is happening in the Universe within each grey band.

The Universe began in an explosion about 13 billion years ago.

The Universe was made of energy that turned into tiny particles of matter within seconds. At this time it was opaque – you could not see through it.

It grew bigger and cooled but remained opaque.

| 0 | 1 trillionth of a second | 1 minute | 1 year | 1,000 years | 300,000 years |

# Changing Universe

The Universe has been changing throughout its entire lifetime. Every aspect of it, such as its size, temperature and structure, has evolved. Only the amount of material in the Universe has remained constant. Even then, this matter has changed in substance. The original elements, hydrogen and helium, have in turn produced all the other elements that now exist. Changes have been on a grand scale and taken billions of years, and they continue today.

The Universe was now cool enough to make atoms and it became transparent.

The atoms started to clump together in cloudy wisps.

Over millions of years clouds formed.

The clouds gradually turned into stars.

By the time the Universe was a few billion years old it consisted of galaxies of stars.

300,000 years

300 million years

1 billion years

3 billion years

### The first stars and galaxies

By about 300,000 years after the Big Bang, the Universe had cooled to roughly 3,000°C. Atoms of hydrogen and helium formed and the Universe became transparent (see-through), as it is today. Very slowly, over the next few million years, the material started to gather and form denser regions. These grew in size over millions more years and developed into thick clouds as more and more material clumped together. Eventually, the clouds formed into balls and became stars. Collections of these stars were the first galaxies.

### The changing face of the Universe

Over the next few billion years, the rest of the galaxies in the Universe formed. Today's galaxies look different from the original ones because there is constant change in the Universe. Galaxies collide and reshape, stars evolve and die, and new stars are born.

### Bigger and bigger

The Universe is getting larger all the time. We know this because the galaxies are still rushing away after the Big Bang explosion. As the Universe expands, it becomes cooler and less concentrated.

### The missing Universe

When we look into space, we detect billions of galaxies and stars scattered through billions of light years. Yet scientists are sure that all we see and know about the Universe is only a fraction of what is there. As much as 95 per cent of the Universe is still to be discovered. This missing part is called dark matter. It was produced along with the other material in the Big Bang – the sort in galaxies and stars. Dark matter is different; it is thought to be tiny particles of energy, much smaller than atoms. But astronomers will only know for sure when the dark matter is found.

▶ Changes on Earth are all part of the continuing change in the Universe. Wind, rain, volcanoes and humans all play their part in altering the Earth's surface. By building cities, such as New York, USA (shown here), people make an enormous difference to the planet.

Galaxies are huge, but they only take up a tiny fraction, less than two millionths, of space.

today

# Home galaxy

It is impossible to know exactly how many galaxies exist. Astronomers estimate that there are about 100–125 billion. There is one galaxy that we know far better than the others. In astronomical terms, it does not stand out from the crowd, but to us it is special. It is the Milky Way, our home galaxy. It consists of at least 500,000 million stars, one of which is our Sun.

◄ The American astronomer Edwin Hubble (1889–1953) was the first person to show that there are galaxies beyond our own, and that they are constantly moving away from the Milky Way.

### Inside the Milky Way
Astronomers believe the Milky Way is a barred spiral galaxy. It is difficult to be sure because we are inside it. All we can see is a mixture of full spiral arms and short segments coming out of a central bulge, but not the Milky Way's complete shape. It is like being inside a forest trying to work out its size and shape, and how many trees it is made of. The Sun is about 25,000 light years from

▼ This is what astronomers think the Milky Way looks like from the outside. It is disc shaped, measuring about 100,000 light years across and about 4,000 light years from top to bottom. The central bulge gets its colour from the many red and yellow old stars it contains. Hotter, younger stars colour the disc blue-white.

▶ Before technology allowed us to understand stars and galaxies as we do today, people used myths and stories to explain what they could see in the sky. In this painting by Tintoretto (1518–1594), the goddess Juno is feeding baby Hercules. According to Roman myth, drops of spilt milk formed the Milky Way.

## Local Group

The Milky Way is part of a cluster of about 30 galaxies called the Local Group. Most of them are small – the biggest are the Milky Way and the Andromeda Galaxy, which is one of the biggest spirals known. It is 2.4 million light years away and is the most distant object that we can see by using just our eyes.

the centre of the Milky Way. From our inside position we get good views of many of the galaxy's individual objects. About 90 per cent of what we can see is stars, and the rest is gas and dust. The dust limits our view of the centre. This is a very active and crowded place and is home to an immense black hole (see page 22), millions of times more massive than the Sun. The stars in the Milky Way orbit (travel around) the centre, all going in the same direction. The Sun completes an orbit every 220 million years.

▲ From our position inside the Milky Way, we can look through it. We see so many stars that their light merges and makes a milky band across our dark sky. The band is broadest and brightest as we look towards the centre of the galaxy (in the middle of this image).

| |
|---|
| 40,000°C |
| 25,000°C |
| 10,000°C |
| 7,000°C |
| 5,500°C |
| 4,500°C |
| 2,000°C |

# Star material

Stars are gigantic, spinning balls of hot, glowing gas that shine throughout the Universe. The one closest to Earth, the Sun, appears huge to us and seems to outshine the rest. At night, we can see many other stars in the sky – small pinpoints of light against the darkness of space. Their huge distance from Earth makes them seem tiny and dim. In fact, some are bigger and brighter than the Sun, while others are smaller and duller. They all have individual characteristics and differ in size, temperature, brightness, colour and mass.

▲ The Sun is by far the brightest star seen from Earth. Its light floods the sky. Other stars become visible only when the Sun is below the horizon and the sky is dark. The Sun is orange-yellow in colour – this means it has a temperature of about 5,500°C.

▲ The hottest stars are blue, the coolest are red. Stars in the night sky all look like pinpoints of white light as they are so far away. To see the star's true colour, astronomers closely examine the light.

### Temperature and colour

All stars are incredibly hot, but some are more so than others. The hottest are about 40,000°C, and the coolest 2,000°C. The colour of a star depends on its surface temperature (see chart above). There are seven main types of star based on colour and temperature.

### Shape, size and mass

All stars are ball-shaped. No stars are star-shaped, nor do any twinkle – they just look like that when their light passes through Earth's atmosphere.

Stars are made of hydrogen gas with some helium, which is pulled into a ball shape by the star's gravity. There is a different quantity of gas in each star. This amount is called the star's mass and it does not change once a star has formed.

Mass is not the same as size: a star with more mass than the Sun is made of more material; a star with a greater size is wider. A big star does not have to be a massive star – it can mean just that its gas is spread out. Some massive stars are very small because their gas is densely packed.

▼ Stars come in a range of sizes. In relation to the Sun, a dwarf star is approximately 100 times smaller; a giant star is typically 30 to 50 times bigger; a blue supergiant is about 100 times bigger; and a red supergiant is up to a few hundred times bigger. The stars below are not shown in their actual position in the sky.

dwarf star (about 8,000°C)

Sun (about 5,500°C)

blue supergiant (over 10,000°C)

▶ Stars shine because of activity in their core, or centre. Deep inside the Sun, hydrogen is being converted to helium, and energy is produced. Much of this energy leaves the Sun as light and heat.

outer layer

inner layer

core

surface
(photosphere)

▲ The Sun is not so bright when seen from Pluto, as in the view above. It looks far dimmer, like a faint point of light, when it is seen from even further away. The reason it looks big to us is that it is very close to Earth.

## Brightness

A star has two sorts of brightness. The first, called 'absolute magnitude', is a measure of the real brightness of a star. It compares the stars as if they were all at the same distance from us. The second measure, called 'apparent magnitude', is the brightness we see from Earth, and compares the stars at their actual, varied distances from us. The Sun is the brightest star on the apparent magnitude scale. But if you lined it up with the other stars all at the same distance, it would look dim.

▶ The two brightest stars in the constellation called Orion are Betelgeuse (top left) and Rigel (bottom right). Betelgeuse is a red supergiant with a surface temperature of about 3,000°C. Rigel's surface temperature is roughly 12,000°C, which means it is a blue-white star.

giant star
(about 4,500°C)

red supergiant
(below 4,500°C)

◀ NASA's *Spitzer Space Telescope* was launched into space by this *Delta* rocket. The telescope has been working in space since 2003, taking photographs of very young stars. The picture of the cloud NGC 7129 on page 19 was taken by this telescope.

# A star is born

Stars are created in enormous clouds of gas and dust inside galaxies. Over hundreds of thousands of years, this gas and dust come together and make hundreds or thousands of mini-clouds. Each of these then develops into a spinning ball of gas, called a protostar – this is the first sign of a new star. In its centre is densely packed gas, which will produce the energy to turn the protostar into a dazzling fully fledged star.

### Switching on a star

Gravity pulls the gas in a protostar towards its centre. As the gas gets more squashed, it gets hotter and hotter. The densest, hottest gas is in the core. When this reaches roughly 10 billion °C, a nuclear reaction starts.

The hydrogen in the core turns into helium, and energy is produced. Two forms of this energy are light and heat. The star has now switched on and will shine steadily for many millions or billions of years.

◄ In the past, before scientists had any alternative theories about star birth, people made up stories explaining how the stars were born. According to Greek mythology, for example, the maiden Callisto, seen here riding a chariot, was turned into a bear by the goddess Artemis. A whirlwind carried her up to the sky where she became the Great Bear constellation.

## Star clusters

Stars are made together in groups called star clusters. A group of young, newly switched on stars is called an open cluster. Often, the stars in the cluster drift apart over millions of years. However, some groups stay together – these are known as globular clusters. The Sun was born in a cluster, probably with a twin star, but the twins and the other stars have drifted apart and now exist alone.

## Lifespan

The length of a star's life is dictated by its mass – the amount of material it is made of. The Sun, and stars of similar mass, live for about 10 billion years. The Sun is about halfway through its lifespan. Stars with greater mass have shorter lives. The most massive last only a few million years. Stars with lower mass have the longest lifespans – they live for many billions of years.

◄ Bright young stars light up the enormous rosebud-shaped cloud of gas and dust that has produced them. There are about 130 young stars in this cloud, known as NGC 7129.

◄ Massive stars are forming inside a gas and dust cloud nicknamed the Papillon. This is in the Large Magellanic Cloud Galaxy, about 170,000 light years from Earth.

# The story of a star

Stars shine steadily for most of their lives. During this time they are called main sequence stars – the Sun is one. As stars get older they change and eventually die. Some stars take millions of years to die and in the process they turn into some of the most beautiful and brightly coloured stars we see in our galaxy. Other stars cut short their lives when they blast themselves across space in one gigantic explosion.

▼ Stars made all the elements in the Universe, such as oxygen and carbon. This means that the elements, which make up all there is on Earth, including human beings, were star material long ago.

## From giant to dwarf

The pattern and length of a star's life and death depend on its mass, the amount of material it is made of. Stars like the Sun and those made of up to about eight times the Sun's mass, all die slowly. This process starts when the star runs out of hydrogen gas to convert into heat and light. It swells, cools and becomes a red giant. Eventually, it pushes off its outer layers of gas, which form a bright and colourful envelope around the dying star. At this colourful stage, the star is called a planetary nebula and it stays like this for tens of thousands of years until the gas disperses in space. Then, all that is left are the remains of the original star, called a white dwarf. This cools, shrinks and dies over billions of years.

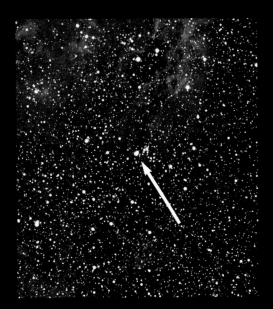

▼ This planetary nebula is nicknamed the Ant because of the shape of its gas. Deep within this, at the centre, is the dying star. It will take tens of thousands of years for the gas to spread out into space and by this time the star will have shrunk, dimmed and cooled.

◄▲ A young, blue star made of about 20 times the mass of the Sun exploded in the nearby galaxy, the Large Magellanic Cloud, in February 1987. The two photographs above show the star before it exploded (left), and the supernova just a few weeks after the explosion (right). Both pictures cover the same area of sky.

## Stellar explosion

Stars that are made of more than eight times the Sun's mass can blow themselves apart in a gargantuan explosion. The star starts off as one of the crowd, but suddenly it explodes and becomes an outstandingly bright and eye-catching new, super star, called a supernova. This can take several months to fade from view. The huge amount of gas and dust it blasts into space is termed a supernova remnant. The core of the original star is left behind after the explosion. Depending on the mass of this core, the star then becomes either a black hole or a neutron star (see pages 22–23).

## Recycling

Material discarded by old stars and blasted off by exploding stars slowly disperses in space. Eventually it comes together with other gas and dust to form enormous clouds, from which new stars take shape over billions of years (see page 18).

# Black holes & neutron stars

Some space objects are not like the usual stars and galaxies. They are far more extreme. For example, a neutron star is only the size of a city but is made of more material than the Sun. It is the smallest and densest kind of star that we can see. At the other end of the scale are galactic black holes. These were made in the young Universe and have been devouring anything that comes too close ever since.

## Galactic black holes

Some galaxies have huge amounts of energy – far more than comes from their stars alone. This power comes from the centre of the galaxy. It is produced by stellar material falling into a galactic black hole, which was formed when the galaxy was born. At that early stage, gravity pulled at the stars and gas at the galaxy's centre. They became so squashed that they collapsed inwards to form an incredibly dense galactic black hole. These have such intense gravity that nothing can ever escape, not even light, which is why the hole is black.

▲ A computer-generated image shows a head-on view of a galactic black hole. This one is at the heart of spiral galaxy, MCG-6-30-15, which is 100 million light years away.

◄ A black hole rips a star apart. The overpowering gravity of the hole pulls at the star's material. It forms a disc of swirling gas before everything disappears into the hole forever.

## Stellar black holes

Smaller, stellar black holes can form from supernova explosions, if the star's core is more than three times the Sun's mass. The core's material is crushed by gravity and collapses inwards. The star gets smaller and denser as it collapses more and more. Eventually, the star is so small and dense, it becomes a hole in space.

▲ A neutron star discovered by its pulses is known as a pulsar. It beams energy into space. The star's magnetic field (turquoise in this computer-generated image) channels the energy into two beams, one on either side of the star.

## Neutrons

Supernova cores which are less than three times the Sun's mass collapse inwards to produce neutron stars. These are unlike any other stars: they are very small in comparison, and have a tough, solid surface. They are also extremely dense – a piece the size of a cherry would weigh over 100 million tonnes on Earth. Like all other stars they spin, but these ones do it super fast – up to several hundred times a second.

▶ The American Robert Oppenheimer (1904–1967) helped us understand neutron stars and black holes. He worked out that neutron stars are always less than about 3 times the Sun's mass.

## Pulsars

Some neutron stars are called pulsars. The star is the same, but a stream of energy is channelled away from it in two beams. As the star spins, its beams sweep around, sending pulses of energy into space. This is much the same as the way a lighthouse sends shafts of light across the sea at night.

# The closest star

There is one star we can see in detail – the Sun. All other stars are light years away, while the Sun is just over eight light minutes from Earth. We can see features on its raging surface – its planet-sized dark spots and its jets and flares of gas shooting into space. The Sun has a family of rock and gas objects, including Earth, that orbits around it. We humans think of the Sun and its family as special. But other stars have planets too.

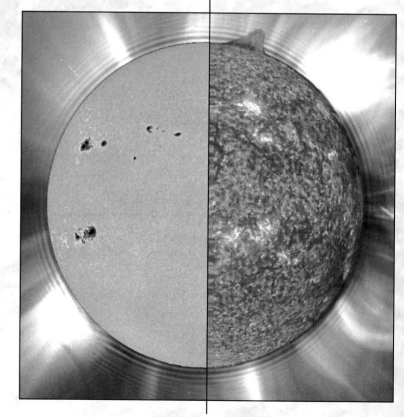

▲ Dark sunspots stand out on the Sun's face. They are cooler areas that appear where hot gas cannot reach the surface. They usually last for weeks at a time.

▲ Great flares and loops of hot gas explode, often over the sunspots (shown on the picture above as white patches). Huge sheets of hot gas extend out from the Sun.

▶ The Sun's energy escapes into space through the surface, which is made of short-lived granules of rising gas. The granules make the Sun's surface resemble orange peel. Each one is about 1,000km across, and they constantly renew themselves.

## The Sun

The Sun is not solid – it is made up of gases. These are mainly hydrogen and helium with tiny amounts of around 90 other elements. Like everything in the Universe, it spins. Unlike Earth, which is rigid and spins as a whole, the parts of the Sun take different amounts of time to spin. The equator takes 25 days and the polar regions over 30 days to rotate once.

The diameter (width) of the Sun is approximately 1.4 million km (about 109 times that of Earth). Its visible surface, the photosphere, is 5,500°C and its core is 15 million °C. Above its surface is its gas atmosphere, which stretches for millions of kilometres into space.

## Stars with planets

When a star is formed, it does not use up all the material in its original cloud of gas and dust. Much is pushed off into space and some can produce planets. The cloud surrounding the star spins and slowly flattens to a disc. This disc material gradually joins together to form planets, which all orbit the star at the centre. We know of over 135 planets orbiting stars outside our Solar System.

## Close stars

The Sun is 149.6 million km away – that is close in space terms. The next nearest star is Proxima Centauri. It is part of a triple star system that includes Alpha Centauri, a double star (two stars that exist together). The three stars are all thought to be 4.3 light years away, but Proxima Centauri is known to be the closest of the three. The 25 next closest stars are all within 12 light years of the Sun.

▶ Although the Sun is the source of light and life for humans, it can also be very damaging. We must never look directly at the Sun – even during a solar eclipse – as the brightness could blind us. We must also be careful when we go out in the Sun – always wear suntan lotion or sunblock and cover up well.

▼ The Sun provides all the energy for life on Earth. Not surprisingly, many cultures, such as the Mayans, who lived in South America about 2,000 years ago, have worshipped the Sun as a god.

# SUMMARY OF CHAPTER 1: A UNIVERSE OF STARS

### Inside the Universe

We have taken our first look into the Universe and found out what it is made of on a grand scale. We have seen that it is full of galaxies and that these exist in every part of the Universe: in nearby space, in the far reaches of space, and everywhere in between. Each one of the galaxies is brimming over with countless stars. We have also discovered that the Universe is huge and it is getting bigger all the time.

The Sun, with a cutaway section showing the core and inner layers

### Going back to the start

For about 70 years, astronomers have known that the Universe is full of galaxies and that it is expanding. These discoveries have made them realize that the Universe was smaller in the past and that the galaxies were once closer together. Over the years, astronomers have pieced together everything they have found out about the stars and galaxies. They now know that the first of these were formed over 12 billion years ago in the young Universe, and that the Universe started about 13 billion years ago with an explosion they call the Big Bang.

### The stellar cycle

The Universe has been constantly changing throughout its lifetime. Not only on a grand scale but in other ways too. Stars exist for only a limited period of time. Like humans, they are born, they change and develop during their lives, and then they die. The gas and dust from which they are made is recycled – the material pushed off by a dying star eventually becomes a part of a new star. The Sun, the closest star to us, is no exception – it is also changing. Deep inside, it is converting hydrogen into helium. This does not make any difference to the way it looks now, but in about 5 billion years' time the Sun will have grown bigger and changed colour. At that stage, it will be a red giant star.

# Go further...

Look deep into the Universe with the *Hubble Space Telescope* at:
www.hubblesite.org

To find out more about the galaxies and stars, including our Sun, go to:
www.jpl.nasa.gov/stars_galaxies

Test your knowledge of the Universe, or have fun building a galaxy at:
http://hubblesite.org/fun_.and._games

If your questions about the Universe are still unanswered, ask an astronomer at: coolcosmos.ipac.caltech.edu/cosmic_kids/AskKids

*To the Ends of the Universe* by Heather Couper and Nigel Henbest (Dorling Kindersley, 1998)

**Astronomer**
Studies the Universe and everything that is in it.

**Astrophysicist**
An astronomer who examines the physics of objects in the Universe.

**Cosmologist**
Looks at the origin, evolution and future of the Universe.

**Galactic astronomer**
Studies the origin, evolution and make-up of galaxies.

**Solar astronomer**
Examines the nearest star, the Sun.

**Stellar astronomer**
Investigates the stars.

Visit a planetarium and watch a projection of the night sky. There are planetaria across the world, e.g. National Space Centre, Exploration Drive, Leicester, LE4, UK
Telephone: +44 (0) 116 261 0261
www.spacecentre.co.uk/home/

The Adler Planetarium and Astronomy Museum has a great exhibition area: 1300 S. Lake Shore Drive, Chicago, USA
Telephone: +1 (0) 312 922 7827
www.adlerplanetarium.org

Book 'an evening with the stars' at The Royal Observatory, Greenwich: National Maritime Museum, Park Row, London, SE10 9NF, UK
Telephone: +44 (0) 20 8312 6565
www.nmm.ac.uk

▶ Jupiter is the largest planet in the Solar System. It is shown here with its moon, Ganymede (below Jupiter in the image), which is the biggest moon in the Solar System.

## CHAPTER 2

# The Sun & its family

A small, bluish ball of rock is our space home. It is the planet called Earth, and it belongs to the Solar System. This is our local space neighbourhood, containing the Sun and its family of planets, moons, spacerocks and comets. This part of space seems enormous to us, but really the Solar System is just a tiny part of one galaxy, the Milky Way, in among millions of galaxies.

The Sun is the biggest, most important central member of our neighbourhood and all the other objects that make up the Solar System follow paths around it. Next in size, after the Sun, come the planets. Some of these are rocky, others are made mainly of gas, several are bigger, others small. But none is covered in water like Earth, nor has life.

Sun
1 Mercury
2 Venus
3 Earth
4 Mars

# Solar System

The Sun and its family are called the Solar System. The Sun, its only star, is the biggest family member, making up about 99 per cent of the Solar System's mass. There are eight main planets, at least three dwarf planets, over 160 moons and trillions of spacerocks and comets. They were all made about 4.6 billion years ago from a cloud of gas and dust, and have been together ever since.

◀ The astronomer William Herschel (1738–1822) discovered the planet Uranus in 1781. Six planets have been known of since ancient times (Mercury, Venus, Earth, Mars, Jupiter and Saturn). Neptune was discovered in 1846 and Pluto (a dwarf planet) in 1930.

▲ Eight main planets (1–8) orbit the Sun. Closest in are the four rock planets: Mercury, Venus, Earth and Mars. Just two of them, Earth and Mars, have moons.

## Family members

The planets form two main groups. The four closest to the Sun – Mercury, Venus, Earth and Mars – are rocky and are known as the rock, or inner, planets. Of these, only Earth and Mars have moons. Then come Jupiter, Saturn, Uranus and Neptune – the gas giants, or outer planets. These huge planets are made mostly of gas, with small, solid rocky centres. They all have moons, and rings of icy rock pieces encircle them.

A ring of spacerocks called the Main Belt, between Mars and Jupiter, separates the two groups. Beyond Neptune is the dwarf planet Pluto, the icy spacerocks of the Edgeworth-Kuiper Belt, and the Oort Cloud, which is made up of comets.

**5**
**Jupiter**

◀ Jupiter is the biggest object in the Solar System after the Sun. It is one of the four gas giants. The others, in order of size and distance from the Sun, are Saturn, Uranus and Neptune. All four are encircled by rings and have families of moons.

**6**
**Saturn**

## Origins

The Solar System was produced from the Solar Nebula, a vast, spinning cloud of gas and dust. The Sun was formed first, then its family. Tiny pieces of material joined to make larger and larger bodies. Material close to the Sun produced the rocky planets – Mercury, Venus, Earth and Mars. The more distant outer planets – Jupiter, Saturn, Uranus and Neptune – were rocky balls at the start. They captured gas, which made enormous atmospheres around their solid cores, and so formed today's gas giants.

## Shape of the Solar System

The Sun is in the centre of the Solar System. Its gravity holds all the other family members in orbit. Each object follows its own path around the Sun and as it travels it spins. The path is its orbit, and a completed circuit is known as one orbit.

The planets all travel around the Sun in the same direction and on a similar plane (flat surface). This means the planetary part of the Solar System is flat and nearly circular. It stretches out about 6 billion km from the Sun.

Comets orbit in any plane, so some comets go above and some go below the Sun. They form a 15 trillion km-wide ball around the planetary part of the Solar System.

**7**
**Uranus**

**8**
**Neptune**

**(9)**
**(Pluto)**

1-4  5  6
7
8  9

▲ All the planets orbit the Sun and they all travel in the same direction, spinning as they go. Pluto has the least circular and the most sloping orbit.

▶ The bright dot in the middle of this image is the planetary part of the Solar System. Surrounding this is the vast ball-shaped cloud of comets, the Oort Cloud.

# Home planet

An extraordinary ball of rock, 12,756km in diameter, lies 149.6 million km from the Sun and speeds around it every 365.25 days, racing along at nearly 30km/sec. This ball is the largest of the rock planets. It has oxygen in its atmosphere and water on its surface. It is a dynamic world bustling with life. Welcome to planet Earth – our home – with its lifeless companion, one quarter of its size, the Moon.

**Earth**
Our home planet has many unique features. It is the only one we know of that has life. The oxygen-rich atmosphere, its second unique feature, supports that life. Living on Earth is comfortable – the average temperature is 15°C, so its third characteristic is that the water can be liquid. In fact, Earth is the only planet with liquid water on its surface. Its fourth unique feature is the crust, the shell of rock covering Earth. It is the only planetary crust that is split into moving parts, or plates, which collide or move apart and renew the surface.

◄ The Moon is easily seen in Earth's sky. It is larger and brighter than any other night-time object. When the side facing us is entirely lit up by the Sun, it is a Full Moon.

▼► The Earth looms large in the Moon's sky. When seen from the Moon, our home planet appears blue because 71 per cent of the surface is covered in water. Unlike the Earth, the Moon's surface has changed little in the past 1.6 billion years or so. The dark areas are the Moon's maria; the lighter areas are older highlands covered in craters.

## The Moon

This dry rock ball was formed about 4.5 billion years ago. A planet-sized rock gave young Earth a glancing blow and splashed material from Earth into space. Slowly, the material came together into a ball, the Moon.

The young Moon was bombarded by spacerocks. As the rocks hit the surface they formed bowl-shaped hollows, called impact craters, many of which can still be seen today. About three billion years ago, lava from volcanoes that were active at the time flooded some of the craters and formed the Moon's enormous plains, called maria.

### Earth–Moon partnership

The Moon travels with Earth around the Sun. The Moon orbits Earth and both spin as they go. Earth spins once every 23.9 hours, the Moon every 27.3 days. It also takes 27.3 days for the Moon to orbit Earth, so the same side – the nearside – always faces us.

The Sun lights both Earth and the Moon – on each, one side is bathed in sunlight when it is night-time on the other side. That is why, on Earth, daytime Australia is night-time Europe.

▲ Many factors shape Earth's landscape – the range of temperatures, types of land, the atmosphere and living things. All in all, we live on a varied and rich planet.

### The shape of the Moon

As the Moon moves around Earth, we see changing phases, or amounts, of it in our sky. To us, the Moon's shape seems to vary between the complete circle of Full Moon and the almost invisible New Moon. What we actually see is the part of the nearside that is lit by the Sun at that time.

# The rock planets

Mercury, Venus and Mars lie close to Earth and they, like our home planet, are balls of rock. The four were made of the same material over the same period of time, but today they are very different worlds. Mercury is a dry, barren planet. Venus is shrouded by a thick blanket of poisonous gas. Frozen, rock-strewn deserts cover cold Mars.

### Atmospheres
Anyone looking at Earth from space can easily see its surface. This is because its atmosphere, the layer of gas covering it, is mostly transparent. Mars has a much thinner atmosphere and Mercury's is almost non-existent. So, we also have a clear view of these planets. Venus is different – a thick atmosphere surrounds it. This stops us seeing Venus' surface, and it also traps in heat from the Sun. This means that Venus has an average temperature of 464°C – it is the hottest planet of all.

▲ The planet Mercury is named after Mercury, the messenger to the Roman gods. The messenger always has wings on his cap.

▼ Mercury's surface is covered by impact craters. It also has cracks, ridges and wrinkles, which were formed when the young hot planet cooled, shrank and its spin slowed.

## Volcanic change

The surfaces of all four rock planets have been changed by volcanoes. With Mercury, this was in the distant past and there are no active volcanoes left today, but on Venus, Earth and Mars changes continued. Venus could be volcanically active again, and we know that our planet is – about 50 volcanoes erupt on Earth each year. The volcanoes on Mars are not expected to erupt again soon, but they may well do so in the future.

## Cratered world

Spacerocks bombarded the rock planets when they were young, about 4 billion years ago. As a rock hit a planet, it formed an impact crater. Most of the craters on Venus, Earth and Mars were destroyed as the surfaces of these planets renewed themselves by, for example, volcanic activity. Mercury still bears the scars of the rock attack as the planet has remained almost unaltered over the years. The only visible changes on Mercury are plains that formed in the distant past when lava from then live volcanoes flowed across its surface.

▲ Mars, like Earth, has white polar caps of ice. The north polar region (1) is easily seen in this view of Mars by the *Hubble Space Telescope*. Further south is the Valles Marineris (2), which cuts across the planet. It is a vast canyon system, 4,500km long and 8km deep.

▼ Venus has more than 1,600 major volcanoes. Maat Mons is one of the largest – it is 9km high with a base 200km across. Solid lava extends for many hundreds of kilometres into the surrounding area.

# Spacerocks

Countless spacerocks travel around the Sun. Most are in the Main Belt, which is an enormous doughnut-shaped racetrack of rocks between Mars and Jupiter. A second, flat belt of icy rock objects, the Edgeworth-Kuiper Belt, lies beyond Neptune. The material in both these belts, and billions more chunks that circle the four giant planets, is leftover material from when the planets were formed.

## The Main Belt

Billions of spacerocks called asteroids make up the Main Belt, also known as the Asteroid Belt. Each cold, dead, rocky, metallic asteroid takes about three to six years to orbit the Sun, spinning every nine hours or so as it goes. At 933km across, circular Ceres is the largest asteroid. Only those bigger than about 320km are round; most are irregular, potato shapes. About a billion or so are between 1km and 250km across, and there are more, smaller still. Yet, the belt is not crowded – thousands of kilometres separate an asteroid from its neighbour.

▲ Eros is 33km long. It started life in the Main Belt of asteroids but now follows a path that crosses over Earth's orbit.

▲ Over 90 per cent of all asteroids (green dots here) are in the Main Belt between the orbits of Mars and Jupiter. Some other asteroids (red dots) follow paths that take them within Earth's orbit. A group of asteroids called the Trojans (small blue dots) travel around the Sun near Jupiter's orbit.

## Planetary rings

The four largest planets – Jupiter, Saturn, Uranus and Neptune – are all encircled by rings. None of the rings are solid bands. Each is a collection of grains, chunks and boulders, which are made of material that ranges from water ice to rock. Saturn's rings contain the most material – at least one million times that of Jupiter's. Its icy pieces reflect the light well and make the rings easy to see.

▲ Gaspra is an asteroid. It is 19km long and orbits the Sun every 3.3 years. It is in the inner edge of the Main Belt.

▶ Saturn's rings look solid but are made of millions of pieces of icy rock, which range in size from dust up to about 5m across. The rings look green in this picture because of the way the photograph was taken. Turn to page 48 to see the rings in true light.

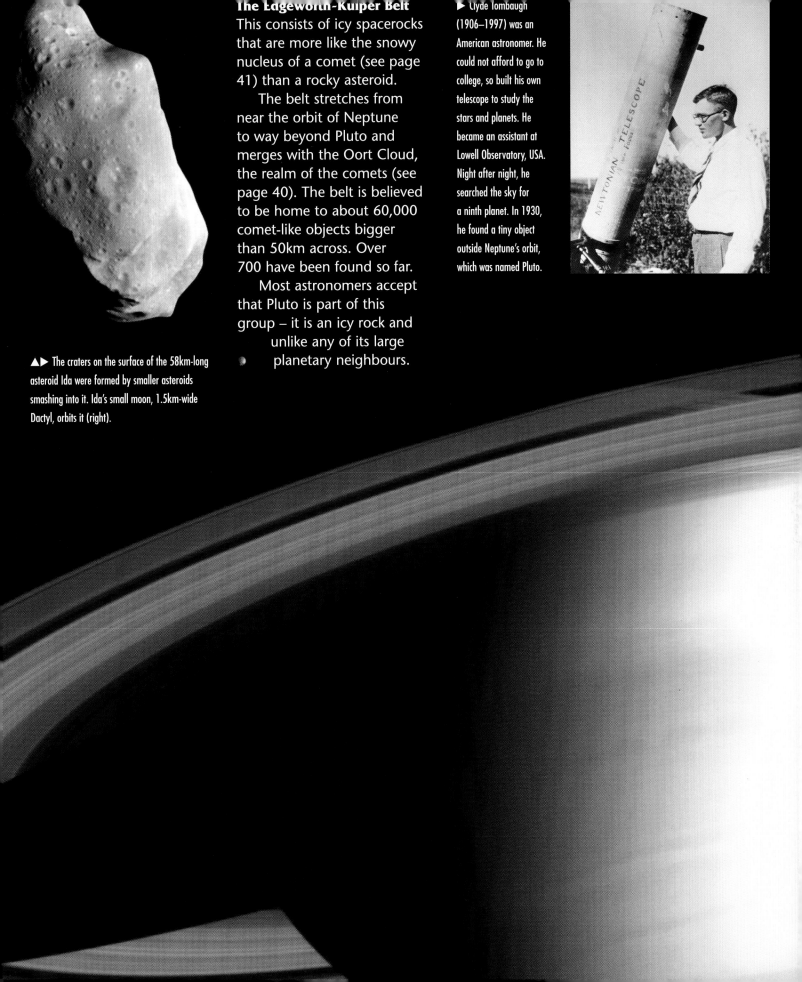

## The Edgeworth-Kuiper Belt

This consists of icy spacerocks that are more like the snowy nucleus of a comet (see page 41) than a rocky asteroid.

The belt stretches from near the orbit of Neptune to way beyond Pluto and merges with the Oort Cloud, the realm of the comets (see page 40). The belt is believed to be home to about 60,000 comet-like objects bigger than 50km across. Over 700 have been found so far.

Most astronomers accept that Pluto is part of this group – it is an icy rock and unlike any of its large planetary neighbours.

▲▶ The craters on the surface of the 58km-long asteroid Ida were formed by smaller asteroids smashing into it. Ida's small moon, 1.5km-wide Dactyl, orbits it (right).

▶ Clyde Tombaugh (1906–1997) was an American astronomer. He could not afford to go to college, so built his own telescope to study the stars and planets. He became an assistant at Lowell Observatory, USA. Night after night, he searched the sky for a ninth planet. In 1930, he found a tiny object outside Neptune's orbit, which was named Pluto.

▼▼ Jupiter, king of the Roman gods and ruler of the heavens, was believed to control storms and is often shown hurling a thunderbolt, as in this Italian painting from the 16th century, and this marble statue. Named after the god, the stormy planet Jupiter is 'king' of the planets because of its enormous size.

# Planetary giants

Four of the planets – Jupiter, Saturn, Uranus and Neptune – have a lot in common: they are giants compared with the other planets and they are all gaseous. They are made mainly of hydrogen and helium, with small amounts of other chemical elements. None of them have solid surfaces and when we look at them, we see their colourful gas atmospheres, but deep below the surface are small round centres of rock. As a result of their size and make-up, these four planetary goliaths are often described as the gas giants.

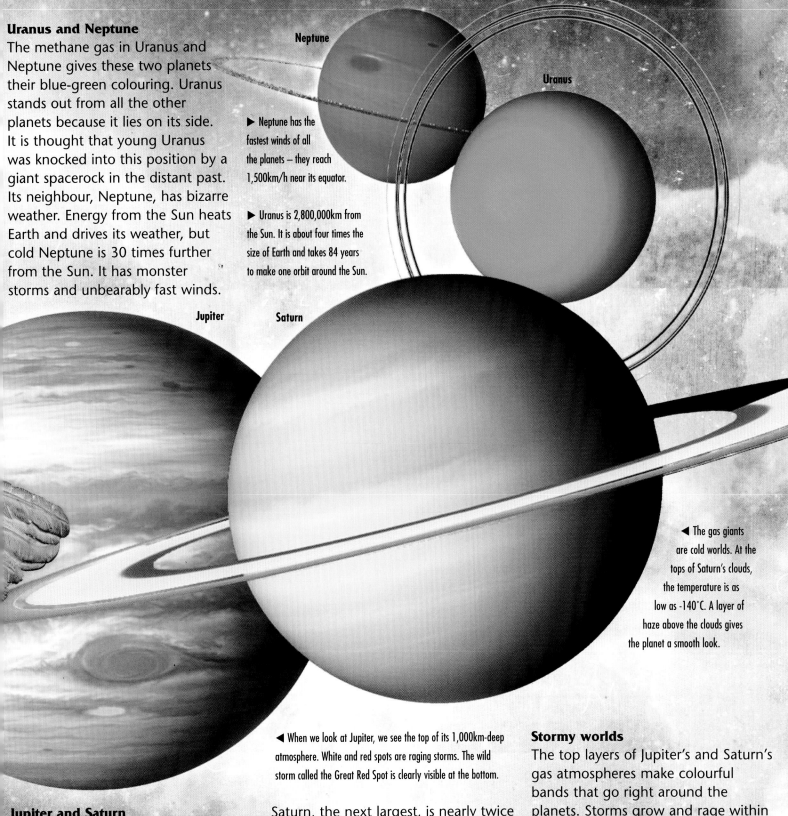

## Uranus and Neptune

The methane gas in Uranus and Neptune gives these two planets their blue-green colouring. Uranus stands out from all the other planets because it lies on its side. It is thought that young Uranus was knocked into this position by a giant spacerock in the distant past. Its neighbour, Neptune, has bizarre weather. Energy from the Sun heats Earth and drives its weather, but cold Neptune is 30 times further from the Sun. It has monster storms and unbearably fast winds.

**Neptune**

▶ Neptune has the fastest winds of all the planets – they reach 1,500km/h near its equator.

▶ Uranus is 2,800,000km from the Sun. It is about four times the size of Earth and takes 84 years to make one orbit around the Sun.

**Uranus**

**Jupiter**

**Saturn**

◀ The gas giants are cold worlds. At the tops of Saturn's clouds, the temperature is as low as -140˚C. A layer of haze above the clouds gives the planet a smooth look.

◀ When we look at Jupiter, we see the top of its 1,000km-deep atmosphere. White and red spots are raging storms. The wild storm called the Great Red Spot is clearly visible at the bottom.

## Stormy worlds

The top layers of Jupiter's and Saturn's gas atmospheres make colourful bands that go right around the planets. Storms grow and rage within the atmospheres of these two planets. A colossal storm on Jupiter, called the Great Red Spot, has been raging and swirling for more than 300 years. No one knows how much longer it might last, but it could well be seen for generations to come.

## Jupiter and Saturn

Jupiter is the biggest giant. The Earth would fit across its face 11 times, and it has a mass 2.5 times that of all the other planets put together. Young Jupiter was even bigger – five times its present size. The planet shrinks by about 2cm a year as it cools.

Saturn, the next largest, is nearly twice as far from the Sun as Jupiter. It is an imperfect ball shape – the region around its equator bulges. Saturn has very clear rings and we get different views of these as the planet orbits the Sun. Sometimes we see them from above and at other times from below.

# Moon families

Six main planets have their own families of moons orbiting them. The four gas giants have big families; Mars has two moons; and Earth has just one. The moons range in size from ball-shaped Ganymede, which is bigger than Mercury, down to the village-sized, potato-shaped lumps, such as Jupiter's Kale. The biggest are worlds in their own right and are as intriguing as any of the planets.

The Italian astronomer Galileo Galilei (1564–1642) observed Jupiter's four largest moons – Io, Europa, Ganymede and Callisto – with the newly invented telescope in 1610. They are now called the Galilean moons because he brought them to other astronomers' and the public's notice.

Io travels above Jupiter's cloud-tops. The image is deceiving: there are 350,000km – roughly 2.5 Jupiters – between the moon and Jupiter's clouds. Io, which is about the same size as Earth's Moon, circles Jupiter every 1.8 days.

### Moon count

There are over 160 moons orbiting the planets. We have known about Earth's Moon ever since the first humans saw it in our night sky; the others have been discovered in the past 400 years. It is likely that all the big moons have been detected, but there are probably a lot of small ones still to be found.

Jupiter has the largest family of moons – it has at least 63. Over 40 of Jupiter's moons have been found since 2000 and more discoveries are expected.

### Origins

The moons of all the planets, apart from Earth, either formed as moons at the same time as their parent planet, or they started off as spacerocks that were captured (pulled in towards the planet by its gravity) sometime in the past. For example, Jupiter's largest moons were made at the same time as the planet, but its smaller ones were originally spacerocks. They travelled a bit too close to Jupiter. As a result, its strong gravity pulled them into an orbit around the planet, where they now still exist as moons.

◄ Io is Jupiter's third largest moon. It is a strange place, unlike anywhere else we know. Volcanoes are erupting on it all the time and, as a result, Io contains some of the hottest parts of the Solar System. The dark green and black marks on the surface, shown here, are all volcanoes. When the volcanoes erupt they can shoot hot gas and dust up to 300km above the surface.

## Contrasting worlds

Over 90 per cent of the moons are less than 500km across. The most recently discovered are smallest of all, just 2 or 3km wide. Those measuring less than about 320km are irregular in shape, but they all look more or less the same – like lumps of barren rock!

The bigger moons are a regular ball shape. The largest is Jupiter's Ganymede, which has a diameter of 5,260km. The moons are made of either rock, such as Ganymede, or a mix of rock and ice, such as Neptune's Triton. Their surfaces are varied – they include cracks, grooves and craters, sulphur lakes, smooth ice plains and ice volcanoes. Only one moon, Saturn's Titan, has a substantial atmosphere – it is completely covered in thick orange clouds.

Oberon

Titania

Umbriel

URANUS

Miranda

Ariel

▲ Five of Uranus' 27 moons are shown with the planet. Titania, the largest, is a bit less than half the size of Earth's Moon. Oberon is a little smaller. Umbriel and Ariel are both about 1,160km across. Cracks and cliffs can be seen on Ariel's surface, and grooves and a large mark on 470km-wide Miranda.

# Dirty snowballs

Far beyond the planets, in the outer reaches of the Solar System, are the comets. They are the most distant objects in orbit around the Sun. There are about ten trillion comets. They are mountain-sized dirty snowballs, usually too small and distant to be seen. Occasionally, one travels close to Earth and it can grow large enough and bright enough to be seen in the sky.

## Cloud of comets

The comets make up the round Oort Cloud, which lies beyond the planetary part of the Solar System. Its inside edge merges with the Edgeworth-Kuiper Belt (see page 35) and its outer edge is roughly 7,500 billion km from us. Comets are a mix of about one third rocky dust and two thirds ice and snow. In 1951, the American astronomer Fred Whipple (1906–2004) described them as dirty snowballs and that is what they have been nicknamed ever since. They have been like this since the Solar System formed 4,600 million years ago.

▶ Halley's Comet is named after Edmond Halley (1656–1742), who realized that the comets seen in 1531, 1607 and 1682 were all the same object. Here, the comet is shown in Earth's sky in 1910, at a time when people still thought that seeing it brought bad luck.

◀ Halley's Comet has been seen in Earth's sky at least 30 times since 240BCE. After seeing the comet in 1301, the Italian artist, Giotto di Bondone (c.1267–1337), showed it as the Star of Bethlehem in his painting, *The Adoration of the Magi*.

▲ An area of trees measuring 30km² was uprooted in the Tunguska region of Siberia, Russia, in an explosion in June 1908. It is believed that the blast was caused by the break-up of a piece of comet, 6km above the ground.

## Travelling comets

Once in a while, a passing star knocks a comet out of the Oort Cloud and into the realm of the planets. Those that travel closer to the Sun than Mars change in a startling way. The Sun heats the comet and turns the snow on its surface to gas. This makes a gassy ball, called a coma, around the snowy nucleus (the dirty snowball part). The coma can grow to 100,000km across. As the comet heats up, gas and dust are pushed away from it and form tails, which are typically 100 million km long. Comets with large comas and long tails are big enough and bright enough to be seen from Earth. About 800 have been seen so far and at least ten more are sighted each year.

▶ The two tails of Comet Hale-Bopp were clearly visible when the comet was in Earth's sky in 1997. The gas tail is narrow and blue, while the broader, white dust tail is slightly curved.

## Reaching Earth

When comets travel through the inner Solar System, they shed large amounts of dust, which Earth can pass through as it orbits the Sun. Tiny bits of the dust, called meteoroids, heat up as they speed through Earth's atmosphere. As they burn, they produce short-lived streaks of light in the sky. These are known to us as shooting stars, or meteors. Thousands of them occur in Earth's atmosphere each year. A really bright meteor is called a fireball. Some meteoroids are rocks which are too big to burn up and they crash onto Earth. These are meteorites.

# SUMMARY OF CHAPTER 2: THE SUN & ITS FAMILY

### Space neighbours

The dominant member of the Solar System is the Sun, our closest star. It is at the centre of the system, and eight planets, at least three dwarf planets, over 160 planetary moons and trillions of spacerocks and comets are kept in orbit around it by its powerful gravity. Each object follows its own path round the Sun, spinning as it goes. All of the space objects were born together, they have lived together for 4.6 billion years and will continue to do so far into the future.

The asteroid Ida

### Solar System family

The four planets closest to the Sun – Mercury, Venus, Earth and Mars – are balls of rock. Beyond them is the Main Belt of asteroids, and then the four biggest planets – Jupiter, Saturn, Uranus and Neptune – which are made mainly of gas. The greater the distance from the Sun, the smaller it appears. The distant planets receive less of its heat and light.

Beyond the main planets is Pluto, which was considered to be a planet from its discovery in 1930 until 2006. Its icy world is now known as a dwarf planet and is known to be one of the largest objects in the Edgeworth-Kuiper Belt.

### Covered by comets

Surrounding the planetary part of the Solar System is an enormous round shell of comets. These objects, described as dirty snowballs, are the most distant members of the Solar System family. When one comes close to Earth, it gives us the chance to see an object in the sky that is normally far beyond our vision.

### Growing family

There is much still to see and discover in the Solar System. The number of objects that we know about goes up each year. Astronomers are sure there are no new main planets to discover, but they expect to find more moons circling the four biggest planets. The astronomers will discover more asteroids and Edgeworth-Kuiper Belt objects, and they will also learn more about the big Solar System objects, such as Jupiter's storms, Mars' rocks and Earth's oceans.

# Go further...

Discover planetary facts:
www.dustbunny.com/afk/planets/

What is your weight on the Moon?
www.exploratorium.edu/ronh/weight

Join a space club at:
spaceplace.jpl.nasa.gov/en/kids/

Test your knowledge of the Solar System at: starchild.gsfc.nasa.gov/docs/StarChild/StarChild.html

*The Earth from the Air for Children* by Yann Arthus-Bertrand (Thames & Hudson, 2002)

*There's No Place Like Space: All about Our Solar System* by Tish Rabe (Random House, 1999)

**Scientist**
Someone who uses the rules and laws of nature to find out more about the world around us. An astronomer uses the rules of science to find out about the Universe.

**Planetary scientist**
Studies the planets of the Solar System, and their moons.

**Planetary geologist**
Looks at the surface rocks and land formations on Mercury, Venus, Earth, Mars and the Moon.

**Cosmogonist**
Examines the origin and general development of the Solar System and other systems of stars with planets.

Go back to 1781 – visit the William Herschel Museum, located in Herschel's home: 19 New King Street, Bath, UK. Telephone: +44 (0) 1225 311 342
www.bath-preservation-trust.org.uk

Visit the Hall of Planet Earth and the Hall of the Meteorites at the American Museum of Natural History: Central Park West at 79th Street, New York, NY 10024-5192, USA Telephone: +1 (0) 212 769 5100
www.amnh.org

Spend an amazing day at Wolfe Creek meteorite crater, Australia: Land Office, Messmate Way, Kununurra 6743, WA Telephone: +61 (0) 8 9168 4200
www.calm.wa.gov.au/national_parks/previous_parks_month/wolfe_creek.html

▶ Aerogel is an extraordinary substance – it is 99.8 per cent air and is 1,000 times less dense than glass. It is being used on the *Stardust* mission to catch particles from a comet.

## CHAPTER 3

# Exploring the Universe

We all like finding things out – about friends, where we live, or faraway places. When we want to discover more about something, we often try to get closer, to look for ourselves. Astronomers spend their lives finding out about the stars and planets. Unfortunately, the stars and most of the Solar System are too far away to be visited. Astronomers study the Universe at long distance – relying on information coming across space to them. This is collected by Earth- and space-based telescopes. Robotic spacecraft are sent to explore Solar System objects and a dozen men have walked on the Moon. Future generations of space travellers will return to the Moon and travel to Mars to explore these worlds for themselves.

◄ A ray of white light is split into its rainbow of colours – its spectrum – as it travels through a glass prism. Astronomers study a star's or a galaxy's light spectrum to find out about that star or galaxy.

# Space detective

**A**stronomers study the Universe. They are interested in everything that is in it, from the planets, stars and galaxies, to how these parts fit together to make the whole. By learning about the Universe today, they learn about its past and how it might develop in the future.

### Looking out

Astronomers are based on Earth, but what they study is billions or trillions of kilometres away – too far for them to travel to. They work at long distance and let information come to them across space.

### Information from space

Stars and galaxies send out information in the form of energy, and one type of energy is light. By collecting this, our eyes make pictures and allow us to see things – our family, a book or a galaxy. Other sorts of energy, such as radio, X-ray, infrared and ultraviolet, are invisible to us. But astronomers' telescopes can collect and make pictures that we can see from these types of energy.

### Starlight

All stars and galaxies have their own light – just as the Sun, our nearest star, provides light. We see other objects, such as planets or moons, by starlight bouncing off their surfaces.

### Looking into the distance

Light lets us see objects in space. As we collect more light by using bigger telescopes, we can see more objects at a greater distance. We learn a lot by looking at the sky with our eyes or a telescope, but close study of the light reveals more information. Astronomers put a special instrument on the end of a telescope to split light into its rainbow of colours – its spectrum. By looking at this, they work out a star's temperature and what it is made of.

▲ If you had eyes that made pictures from infrared energy rather than light energy, this is what a pair of feet in trainers would look like. Infrared is mainly heat energy. It is given off by anything with a temperature. In this image, the hottest parts of the feet are coloured red, warm parts are yellow, then cooler areas go through green and blue to mauve (coldest).

## Complete picture

Light tells us a lot about an object but not everything. Big chunks of some galaxies are invisible because we get no light from them, so we detect the region by its radio energy.

Elsewhere, whole objects are only detected by energy other than light. Young, dim stars are invisible next to brighter stars, others are hidden by dust clouds. These stars are detected by their infrared energy.

A black hole gives off no light, but we know it exists because of the X-ray energy around the hole.

Astronomers collect all the different types of energy to get as complete a picture as possible of the Universe.

▼ Astronomers collect a range of energy from the galaxy M81. The images below show it in radio energy (top), infrared energy (bottom left), visible light (bottom centre), and ultraviolet energy (bottom right). Each view shows different details of the galaxy's core of old stars and its spiral arms full of young, hot stars.

# Collecting information

Telescopes collect light and other types of energy from objects in space. An individual telescope usually collects just one sort, such as light, infrared or X-ray energy. Whatever the type, all telescopes work in much the same way: collecting the energy, recording it, and then using it to make images and to find out about the stars and planets. Earth's atmosphere stops some types of energy reaching our planet's surface. That is why some telescopes work in space, whilst others are based on Earth.

▲ A hexagonal piece of telescope mirror is cleaned to remove dust from its surface. The 10m-wide *Keck* mirror is made from 36 mirror pieces, like this one, fitted together.

▶ The world's largest individual telescopes are on top of a volcano in Hawaii. They are the twin telescopes, *Keck I* and *Keck II*, and have been used since the mid-1990s. Each is about 25m tall and is protected by a dome (right). Another ten top-class telescopes occupy the same site.

*XMM-Newton*

▼ These two telescopes, the European *XMM-Newton* and the American *Chandra*, work in space near Earth. They collect X-ray data about distant structures such as black holes and galaxies.

*Chandra*

▲ The *Spitzer Space Telescope* is prepared for its launch in 2003. It collects infrared energy. The telescope has chilling systems to keep it cool. Without them, it would record its own heat energy instead of that of the planets, stars and galaxies it studies.

## Telescopes on Earth

The biggest and best light-collecting telescopes on Earth are on mountain tops. Light gets through Earth's atmosphere all the way to sea level, but the mountain-top sites are above the clouds and away from city lights. The air is thin, dry and still, allowing astronomers to get a great view of the Universe. The telescopes are inside domes and several can occupy the same location – together they form an observatory.

Radio telescopes can also be found on Earth – they are usually on lower, flat ground, as radio waves make it through Earth's atmosphere.

## Telescopes in space

While astronomers have been using telescopes on Earth for nearly 400 years (see page 38), they have only been looking at the Universe through space-based telescopes for about 40 years. Space telescopes are used to collect the types of energy, such as X-ray energy, that cannot get through Earth's atmosphere. These minibus-sized telescopes orbit the Earth looking out into space. They collect and record information 24 hours a day, all year round, whatever the weather.

▼ You do not have to be an expert astronomer to enjoy the Moon, planets and stars in the sky. You can see plenty with your eyes alone, and binoculars or a telescope will show you even more. It is a fascinating Universe, so why not take a look at the sky at night?

## Using the information

Computers are really important to astronomers. They are used to work telescopes; they record and store information from space; and they help astronomers study the findings. No one needs to be near a telescope to operate it, whether it is based on Earth or in space. Information is sent to a control room and from there it is forwarded to the astronomer's own computer. These scientists live all over the world – many work in universities or for government organizations. They use the data from the stars and planets to help us understand and appreciate our Universe.

# Space robots

**R**obots have been exploring space for us for the past 40 years or so. They are not human-shaped robots but car-sized spacecraft consisting of a framework with tools attached. They are called space probes and each is designed to explore a specific target, such as the Moon or Saturn. Some shoot past their targets, taking and recording information as they fly by. Some go into orbit around these distant worlds, and others land on them.

▲ *Genesis* completed its three-year mission in 2004. This involved travelling towards the Sun, collecting samples of its solar wind – atoms of the Sun in space – and returning these to Earth.

◄ The solar wind collected by *Genesis* was stored in a capsule. To try to make sure this container survived the journey back to Earth, a clever retrieval plan was devised. As you can see in the test run pictured here, a parachute slowed the capsule's fall. A long pole beneath a helicopter was then supposed to catch the container and carry it to the ground.

◄ Sadly, the retrieval plan did not work and *Genesis'* capsule crashed into the desert in Utah, USA, on 8 September 2004. Its parachutes failed to open and the container smashed into the ground at about 310km/h. However, all was not lost – some of the solar-wind atoms survived.

▲ It took seven years for *Cassini* to reach Saturn. On its arrival, in July 2004, it went into orbit around the planet and started a four-year study of Saturn, its rings and moons. It will complete 74 orbits and make 44 close fly-bys of Titan and other moons such as Enceladus and Dione.

### Reaching the target

Space probes start their journey by rocket or, very occasionally, by space shuttle. The United States has built the most probes. The Soviet countries sent many in the past, and now Japan and Europe explore space this way.

Probes are sent to many types of Solar System object – they have been to all the eight main planets, and they have investigated the Sun, moons, comets and asteroids.

### Profile of a space probe

Space probes can look very different from each other and come in a range of sizes and shapes, depending on their goal. But they all have things in common. Each probe has a power source, and a computer to control the mission and to deal with the data it collects. A communications system sends and receives messages, and a set of tools and instruments is there to investigate the target.

### Cassini at work

One of the largest and most complex space robots ever built, *Cassini* is the fourth probe to investigate Saturn. American *Cassini* gave a ride to *Huygens*, a smaller European probe, which is designed to descend by parachute through the murky atmosphere of Titan, and down to the moon's surface. Between them, they carry 18 instruments, tools and cameras to find and record data.

▼ Aerogel (see page 43) is on board the *Stardust* probe – the first-ever mission to collect comet particles. It is a sponge-like solid which is made of 99.8 per cent air. It is an excellent insulator against heat – that is why the crayons, which are lying on the aerogel in the picture, are not melting despite being heated.

# Landers & rovers

Space robots have landed on the Moon, Venus, Mars, and on the asteroid Eros. Once on the surface, the probes – called landers – switch on, look around and then investigate. Some move about, others stay still. The landers work while they have power – this can be for months. When their job is over, they stay forever on their new home.

## Getting there

One of the trickiest parts of a lander's mission is arriving safely. It needs to slow down after its supersonic journey from Earth. The aim is a soft, controlled landing rather than a crash. This is done using small rockets; parachutes, if there is an atmosphere; or blow-up balls to cushion the lander's fall and bounce it to a halt. Scientists on Earth are in contact as the lander comes down. Its landing site is always carefully chosen, but the exact location of the touchdown is unknown until the lander has stopped.

▲ This computer chip is on board the Mars rover *Opportunity*. It has about 35,000 laser-engraved signatures on it. These are from people who visited *Spirit* and *Opportunity* as they were built.

▶ The camera high up on *Spirit*, the Mars rover, surveys the landscape, looking for interesting rock or soil sites for the craft to move to. The 'rat' (rock abrasion tool) on the tool arm (near the front wheels) scrapes away the top layers of a rock to see beneath.

▲ Seven *Surveyor* landers were sent to the Moon between 1966 and 1968. Two crash landed, the other five, including *Surveyor 3* (above), landed safely, took pictures and tested the surface for the astronauts who would follow. *Apollo 12* landed (on horizon) near *Surveyor 3*, in November 1969.

## Standing still

Some landers investigate just in the place of landing – they do not move about. The most successful lander missions were some of the *Surveyor* probes on the Moon in the 1960s and the two *Viking* landers on Mars in 1976.

Others missions have landed on Venus and on Eros. Between 1970 and 1982, eight *Venera* craft survived the journey through its thick atmosphere to land on Venus. In 2001, *NEAR* studied Eros from above its surface. Once this job was done, the craft landed on the asteroid – an added bonus to its mission.

## Roving around

Landers that move about are nicknamed rovers. Five rovers have been sent into space. Two *Lunokhod* craft worked on the Moon in the 1970s. *Sojourner* travelled across Mars in 1997 and, in 2004, *Opportunity* and *Spirit* did the same. These twin rovers used a camera and tools to study rocks and soil, and look for signs of liquid water on Mars in the past.

1. *Tumbleweed*, a new rover, is currently being tested for use on planets and moons. It is an inflated ball containing instruments. Here, the wind-blown rover is bouncing along.

2. *Tumbleweed* comes to a stop at an area of scientific interest on the planet it is investigating. Once it has reached a standstill, the rover deflates.

3. Now you can see a cutaway diagram of the rover. At this stage, instruments and a drill are used to take measurements and samples from the surface.

4. *Tumbleweed* transmits information to an orbiting satellite which sends the data back to Earth. Once finished, the rover reinflates itself and sets off again on its journey.

# Life search

There are billions of living things in the Universe. Humans are just one kind; many more creatures and plants live on land and in water. Some are single-celled structures, others are multi-billion-celled intelligent beings. All have one thing in common – they live on planet Earth. As far as we know there is no life outside Earth. Most astronomers believe it is there and some are searching for it. But, for now, its form and home remain a mystery.

◄ Some astronomers once thought intelligent creatures lived on Mars. This 1936 comic shows how one artist imagined extraterrestrial life. Today's cartoons continue to fantasize about strange-looking aliens.

► Life is found in unexpected places on Earth, and it survives extreme conditions. This sea anemone is living 3.5km below the surface, where there is no light.

▼ Life on Earth became land-based about 400 million years ago. Humans, the dominant form of life on Earth, have been around for about 2 million years.

## Life on Earth

There has been life on Earth for about 3.8 billion years – that is over three quarters of the planet's lifetime. It started with single-celled ocean life. This evolved into complex plants and animals, in Earth's oceans and on land. Today, life is found in all sorts of places. By studying it, we have learned what life outside Earth needs to get started and to survive, and where it might be. We are looking in places that have liquid water, carbon (the most common atom in living things), other elements such as nitrogen, and energy such as sunlight or lightning.

## Life elsewhere in the Solar System

Mars is not suitable for life today, but it may have been home to primitive life in the past. Its water is frozen now, but about 3.5 billion years ago it was liquid. Perhaps life developed in Mars' water as it did in Earth's.

In 1976, two space probes tested Mars' surface for indications of life; none were found. Future probes to Europa and Mars may find signs of life. Saturn's moon, Titan, was once thought inhospitable, but the discovery of life in harsh conditions on Earth means this moon is another place where life might exist.

▼ This computer-generated image shows what Mars might have looked like 3.5 billion years ago. A river of water cuts through the rocky landscape, and the Sun shines in the martian sky.

▲ *Darwin* is a group of eight spacecraft. Six of the craft are space telescopes, the seventh combines the light collected by all of the telescopes. The eighth will communicate with Earth and the rest of the group. Together they will scan the nearby Universe for worlds like Earth and then look for gases that could indicate signs of life.

## Beyond the Solar System

Astronomers are searching for primitive life in the Solar System – anything sophisticated would have been found by now. But the search beyond is very different.

Our galaxy has thousands of planets and moons that are capable of harbouring life. Perhaps one is like Earth and home to someone like you. Finding out is not easy – the nearest star with planets is beyond our reach. A space probe would take billions of years to get there. But intelligent life makes noise. We have been listening for noise signals for about 40 years, but have heard nothing – yet.

# Journey of a lifetime

A trip into space is one of the most exciting and memorable things that a human can do. About 400 men and women have made the trip, and there are plenty more eager to follow. Nearly all of the astronauts have gone into space immediately around Earth. Just 26 have ventured further, to our Moon. In the decades ahead, we will go further still. For now, we are just discovering what it is like to live and work away from our familiar home on Earth.

▲ Astronauts aboard the International Space Station (ISS) have to cope without the help of gravity — even simply moving about is a challenge. The weightless conditions affect the human body: in this picture, André Kuipers wears equipment that records changes in his body as he moves about.

## Space and the human body

The human body is designed to live on Earth – we breathe oxygen, live in warm temperatures and are used to the pull of gravity. It is different a few hundred kilometres above our planet where astronauts live and work. Here, where they do not feel gravity's pull, they are weightless and float about. The temperature is either high enough to toast them, or low enough to freeze them, and there is no oxygen. They are safe inside their craft but need the protection of spacesuits once outside.

Most feel sick at the beginning of a trip. This does not last, but some discomfort lingers. In the weightless environment, body fluids are not pulled downwards by gravity and this can feel strange. The heart does not have to pump so hard to get blood around the body, the nose gets blocked and faces become puffy. The important thing is to eat well and exercise to stay fit and healthy.

### Men on the Moon

Of the 26 American men who travelled to the Moon in six missions between 1969 and 1972, 12 walked on its surface and all returned home. The 12 took photographs, collected 388kg of rock and soil, and set up experiments. No one has been back since, but there are plans to return.

▼ The *Lunar Roving Vehicle* was used on three Moon missions. American Eugene Cernan, seen here, was commander of *Apollo 17*, the final mission. He was the last man to walk on the Moon.

bit by bit since the first piece arrived in space by rocket in 1998. Later pieces, crew and supplies have been ferried to the ISS by space shuttles and rockets. Crew have lived on board since 2000.

### Target Mars

Mars is the next new place humans will visit. We are not going there just yet – we need a new vehicle for the journey and we are still learning about the planet. A trip to Mars and back would last about three years, so we need to know that a crew could cope over such a long time.

For the time being, astronauts are staying closer to Earth – on board the ISS, which orbits our planet. All they learn here about life in space will help put them a step closer to Mars.

▼ A spacesuit provides oxygen for breathing and keeps an astronaut's temperature at a safe level. American Rex Walheim wears his as he works outside the ISS in April 2002.

◄ Before this century is over, you may become a space tourist, staying in a holiday city orbiting Earth. What you would find there is a series of linked hotels and leisure areas. You would spend the night in a fixed sleeping bag to stop you floating about. In the day, you could leap about in the gymnastics hall, or simply admire the view from an observation gallery where artificial gravity would help you stay still.

# The future

Astronomers know a lot about the Universe, yet they realize there is still plenty to learn. They would like to answer questions about worlds local to Earth, such as, what is Pluto really like, and was there ever life on Mars? They would also like to know more about the distant galaxies and stars. A fresh breed of telescopes and spacecraft will help the astronomers make new discoveries and answer their questions. In the far future, humans living on the Moon or Mars will uncover new information themselves.

▲ At the moment, we can send only rovers to Mars. But it is possible that within 50 years, astronauts will travel to this planet.

### Telescopes of the future

Bigger and better telescopes will help astronomers see more of the Universe in the decades ahead. The bigger a telescope is, the more and further astronomers see. Ones that have large, single mirrors that sag are unusable. Future mirrors will be made of many, smaller pieces, allowing huge telescopes to be built. Astronomers will also link telescopes across Earth. These will be able to work together to show us more of the Universe.

### Space probes of the future

Astronomers and space scientists are constantly planning future missions and new space probes. Pluto, Mars and Jupiter's moon, Europa, are already in their sights. A future aim is to bring back pieces of planets and moons to Earth for study.

The stars are too far away for a space probe mission at the moment. But engineers are working on ideas for faster craft. In the far future, we may reach out of our Solar System.

### Humans in space

New vehicles to take humans to Mars and the Moon are being designed. Today's astronauts will be too old to carry out the work planned. They are relying on future generations to carry on where they left off. Will yours be the first human footprint on Mars?

▶ The *James Webb Space Telescope* is being prepared to take over from the *Hubble Space Telescope*, which is in space now. It will work for about ten years and then be replaced by another telescope.

# SUMMARY OF CHAPTER 3: EXPLORING THE UNIVERSE

### Curiosity

Humans have always been curious about where they live. Not just about Earth but about what lies further out, in our Solar System and beyond. People have been learning about the Universe for thousands of years. At first, they used just their eyes. Then about 400 years ago, they turned the newly invented telescope upwards. It soon revealed unimagined wonders: worlds never seen before, such as Jupiter's moons and stars galore.

The *Genesis* probe collected samples of particles of solar wind.

### Tools of exploration

The telescope has been the astronomer's basic tool since it was first used. Today's telescopes are enormous – they see much further and in more detail, but like the first, they collect light from the stars and planets and form it into pictures. Telescopes are now based on Earth and in space, and they also collect other sorts of energy, such as radio, X-ray or infrared energy. All types of information are used to give us a better understanding of the Universe.

### Robotic craft

Space probes regularly explore Solar System objects for us. They make discoveries, and show us new and familiar objects in close-up. Without them we would not know what the planet Neptune or a comet's nucleus look like, nor understand what it is like on the surface of Mars.

### The astronomer

The telescopes and space probes are important because they collect information from space. But a third tool, the astronomer's brain, is essential. The astronomer analyzes the information to find out more about the Universe. When results have been examined and conclusions drawn from data we have available, the astronomer decides what new questions we would like to answer and how we will do this in the future.

# Go further...

Read about the ISS: space flight.nasa.gov/station

Learn more about the spacecraft in the Solar System at: www.jpl.nasa.gov/solar_system

Download models of spacecraft to build: www.jpl.nasa.gov/scalemodels

Like to be an astronaut? www.esa.int/e saHS/ESA1RMGBCLC_astronauts_0.html

Try out some training exercises at: edspace.nasa.gov/text/astroschool/

*Space Exploration* by Carole Stott, (Dorling Kindersley, 2004)

*Stargazing: Astronomy without a Telescope* by Patrick Moore (CUP, 2000)

**Space scientist**
Works with spacecraft.

**Astronaut**
Man or woman who travels to space.

**Telescope operator**
Operates Earth-based or space-based telescopes on behalf of astronomers.

**Astrobiologist**
Someone who studies the origin and evolution of life.

**Radio astronomer**
Collects radio data from space and uses it to learn about the Universe.

**Astrophotographer**
Takes photographs of the night sky and of individual objects in it.

Visit the Kennedy Space Center where you can walk around spacecraft and question an astronaut.
Kennedy Space Center, Florida, USA
Telephone: +1 (0) 321 449 4444
www.kennedyspacecenter.com

Get up close to spacecraft at the Cité de l'Espace space park:
Avenue Jean Gonord,
31506 Toulouse, France
Telephone: +33 (0) 5 62 71 56 05
www.cite-espace.com

Learn more about living in space at:
The Science Museum
Exhibition Road
London, SW7 2DD, UK
Telephone: +44 (0) 870 870 4868
www.sciencemuseum.org.uk

# Glossary

**absolute magnitude**
A measure of the true brightness of a star.

**amateur**
Someone who does something as a hobby. An amateur astronomer is someone who studies the stars and planets in their leisure time.

**apparent magnitude**
A measure of the brightness of a star seen from Earth.

**asteroid**
A spacerock orbiting the Sun. Most asteroids are in the Main Belt.

**astronaut**
A person who travels into space.

**astronomer**
A person who studies the Universe and everything in it, beyond Earth.

**astronomy**
The study of everything in space – all space objects and space itself.

**atmosphere**
Gases held around a planet or moon by its gravity. A star's atmosphere is the gas held beyond its photosphere.

**atom**
The smallest part of an element.

**Big Bang**
The explosion that scientists believe created our Universe, space and time, about 13 billion years ago.

**billion**
One thousand million (one followed by nine zeros).

**brightness**
A measure of a star's light.

**cluster**
A group of galaxies or stars held together by gravity.

**comet**
A small snow, ice and dust object, nicknamed a dirty snowball.

**constellation**
A piece of sky where bright stars form an imaginary pattern such as that of a human or an animal.

**crater**
A bowl-shaped hollow on the surface of a planet, moon or asteroid formed by a spacerock crashing into it.

**dark matter**
The material in the Universe that it is not possible to find; it makes up as much as 95 per cent of the Universe.

**Edgeworth-Kuiper Belt**
The flat belt of icy spacerocks beyond the orbit of Neptune.

**element**
A basic substance of nature such as hydrogen, oxygen and carbon.

**ellipse**
A two-dimensional shape; a long circle.

**equator**
An imaginary line drawn around the middle of a planet, moon or star. It divides the top (northern) half from the bottom (southern) half.

**fireball**
A very bright meteor.

**fly-by**
A space probe that journeys to a planet or moon and then records information as it flies past its target. 'Fly-by' is also used to describe this type of mission.

**galactic black hole**
A massive, dense hole in space at the centre of a galaxy.

**galaxy**
A vast collection of stars, gas and dust held together by gravity.

**gas giants**
The four largest planets, which are made mainly of gas – Jupiter, Saturn, Uranus and Neptune.

**globular cluster**
A ball-shaped group of old stars that exist together.

**gravity**
A force of attraction. The Sun's gravity pulls on Earth, Earth's gravity pulls on you.

**hexagonal**
A six-sided shape.

**lava**
Molten (hot, liquid) rock that flows out of a planet or moon (see **volcano**).

**light year**
A unit used to measure distances across the Universe. One light year is the distance light travels in one year.

**magnetic field**
Region of space around a planet or star, where the magnetism produced by the planet or star is felt.

**Main Belt**
The doughnut-shaped belt of asteroids between Mars and Jupiter.

**maria (singular: mare)**
Dark markings on the Moon – large depressions in the surface which were flooded by volcanic lava in the past.

**mass**
The amount of material in an object. A star of 8 solar masses has 8 times the amount of material in the Sun.

**meteor**
The streak of light produced by a meteoroid as it travels through Earth's atmosphere.

**meteorite**
A spacerock that lands on Earth, another planet or a moon.

**meteoroid**
A tiny piece of dust from a comet or asteroid.

**Milky Way**
The galaxy we live in. Also, the name of the path of stars seen in Earth's sky.

**million**
One thousand thousand (one followed by six zeros).

**moon**
A rock, or rock and ice body that orbits around a planet or an asteroid.

**nebula**
A cloud of gas and dust in space.

**neutron star**
A small, densely-packed star produced in a supernova explosion.

**nuclear reaction**
The process that takes place inside a star when elements are changed to other elements.

**observatory**
A building or group of buildings that house telescopes.

**Oort Cloud**
The huge shell of comets around the planetary part of the Solar System.

**opaque**
Foggy; not allowing light to pass through; not see-through.

**open cluster**
A group of young, bright stars, which will eventually drift apart.

**orbit**
The path one object takes around another, more massive object. The Moon orbits Earth and Earth orbits the Sun.

**photosphere**
The visible layer of a star, e.g. the Sun.

**planet**
A large, round body made of rock or gas that orbits a star.

**planetary nebula**
A type of star. It consists of an expanding, colourful cloud of gas and dust, which has been ejected by the dying star at the centre of the cloud.

**professional**
Someone who does something as their job. A professional astronomer is paid to study the stars and planets.

**protostar**
A very young star.

**pulsar**
A neutron star which is identified by its beams of energy. The energy pulses across space as the star spins.

**ring system**
A collection of rings around a planet.

**rock planets**
The four planets closest to the Sun – Mercury, Venus, Earth and Mars. Also called the inner planets.

**satellite**
An object held in orbit around a planet or moon by gravity. A telescope in orbit around Earth is a man-made satellite. The Moon is a natural satellite of Earth.

**solar eclipse**
The effect achieved when the Moon is between the Sun and Earth, and the Moon's shadow falls on Earth.

**Solar Nebula**
The spinning cloud of gas and dust that formed into the Solar System.

**Solar System**
The Sun and all the objects that orbit

it: nine planets, over 140 moons, spacerocks and comets.

**solar wind**
A stream of the particles blown away from the Sun that make up the Sun's atoms.

**space probe**
A type of spacecraft, also called a probe. An unmanned, robotic craft sent to look at Solar System objects.

**spacerock**
A small rock or icy rock object that orbits the Sun.

**spectrum**
The rainbow band of colours produced when light is split.

**star**
A ball of hot, bright gas that produces energy by nuclear reaction.

**stellar**
Of or like a star.

**stellar black hole**
The remains of a star that has collapsed in on itself.

**sunspot**
A dark, cool patch on the surface of the Sun.

**supercluster**
A number of clusters of galaxies held together by gravity.

**supernova**
A massive star that has suddenly exploded and shines brightly.

**supernova remnant**
The gas and dust remains of a supernova explosion.

**telescope**
An instrument that uses lenses, mirrors or a combination of the two, to collect light from a distant object and form that light into an image. Telescopes also collect radio, X-ray, infrared and ultraviolet energy.

**trillion**
One million million (one followed by 12 zeros).

**Universe**
Everything that exists – all of space and everything in it.

**volcano**
Mountains made of material that started off inside a planet. Molten rock (lava) bursts through the planet's crust and flows onto its surface, building a volcano in the process.

# Index

# Acknowledgements

The publisher would like to thank the following for permission to reproduce their material. Every care has been taken to trace copyright holders. However, if there have been unintentional omissions or failure to trace copyright holders, we apologize and will, if informed, endeavour to make corrections in any future edition.

Key: *b* = bottom, *c* = centre, *l* = left, *r* = right, *t* = top

pages: front cover (*left to right*) NASA/Hubble Space Telescope, NASA/JPL, Science Photo Library/NASA; 1 Science Photo Library/Jerry Lodriguss (SPL); 2 SPL/NASA; 4–5 NASA; 7*t* SOHO/NASA; 8*bl* Corbis/Bill Varie; 8–9*t* NASA/ESA/S.Beckwith(STScI)/HUDF Team; 9*cl* SPL/Royal Observatory, Edinburgh; 9*cr* NASA/JPL; 9*bl* STScI/AURA; 9*br* SPL/NOAO; 10*bl* Corbis/Bettmann; 10*tr* Galaxy Picture Library/Robin Scagell 11*tl* Galaxy /Robin Scagell; 11*tc* SPL/Celestial Image; 11*tr* SPl/NASA/Space Telescope Science Institute; 13*br* Corbis/David Zimmerman; 14*l* Corbis/ Bettmann; 15*tr* National Gallery, London; 15*br* SPL/Eckhard Slawik; 16*tr* Getty Imagebank; 17*tl* Galaxy/Robin Scagell; 17*cr* Alamy/Photo Network; 18*l* NASA; 18–19 Bridgeman Art Library/ Villa Farnesina, Rome; 19*tr* SPL/ Pekka Parviainen; 19*bl* NASA/JPL; 20*l* Galaxy/Swedish Solar Vacuum Telescope; 20–21*bc* SPL/NASA/ Space Telescope Institute; 21*tc* and *tr* David Malin Images/Anglo-Australian Observatory; 22*bl* SPL/David Hardy; 22–23*t* SPL/NASA; 23*tr* SPL/Russell Kightley; 23*br* Corbis; 24–25 NASA/Stefan Seip; 24*br* SOHO/NASA; 25*cl* Galaxy Swedish Solar Vacuum Telescope; 25*bc* Bridgeman Art Library/Private Collection; 25*br* Corbis/Galen Rowell; 27 SPL/NASA; 28*bl* Corbis/Bettmann; 29*br* Galaxy/Calvin J. Hamilton; 30*cl* Corbis/Brian Vikander; 30–31*b* Alamy/Goodshoot; 31*tc* Corbis/Peter Turnley; 31*c* Getty Imagebank; 31*cr* Corbis/Jonathan Blair; 32*tl* Corbis/Araldo de Luca; 32*bl* NASA/JPL; 32–33 SPL/NASA/SMU/David P. Anderson; 33*tr* NASA; 34*cl* Galaxy/Gareth Williams; 34*c* Galaxy/NASA; 34*cr* Galaxy/NASA; 35*tl* Galaxy/NASA; 35*tr* Corbis/Bettmann; 35*br* NASA/JPL; 36*tl* Art Archive/Palazzo de Te Mantua/Dagli Orti; 36*br* Corbis/Araldo de Luca; 38*tl* Corbis; 38*bl* NASA/JPL; 39*tl* NASA/Steve Lee, Jim Bell, Mike Wolff; 39*b* SPL/NASA; 40*bl* Art Archive/Scrovegni Chapel, Padua/Dagli Orti; 40*tr* Corbis/Bettmann; 40*br* Novosti News Agency, London; 41 Galaxy/Robin Scagell; 42*tl* Galaxy/NASA; 43 NASA/JPL; 44*tl* SPL/David Parker; 44–45 SPL/Sir Arthur Tucker; 45*bc* and *bl* NASA/JPL; 45*cr* and *br* NASA/UIT; 46*tl*, and 46–47 Corbis/Roger Ressmeyer; 47*tl* NASA/SCOPE; 47*tc* European Space Agency (ESA); 47*tr* ESA/NASA; 47*bc* Corbis/Gabe Palmer; 48*tl* NASA/JPL; 48*cl* SPL/NASA; 48*bl* SPL/NASA; 48–49 ESA; 49*br* NASA/JPL; 50*bl* SPL/NASA; 50*tr* NASA/JPL; 50–51 NASA/JPL; 51*tr* NASA/JPL (x4); 52*tl* Art Archive/Eileen Tweedy; 52*bl* Corbis/Bill Ross; 52*cr* SPL/B. Murton; 53*tl* ESA; 53*tr* SPL/ESA; 53*b* SPL/Kees Veenenbos; 54*tl* ESA; 54–55 SPL/NASA; 55*tc* NASA; 55*br* NASA; 56–57 SPL/Victor Habbick; 57*tr* NASA; 57*br* NASA; 58*tl* NASA/JPL; 59*br* NAA/JPL; 60*bl* SPL/NASA; 61*tr* NSF/AURA/NOAO; 64*bl* Alamy/Imagestate

The publisher would like to thank the following illustrators: Julian Baum (14–15, 29. 37), Mark Bristow (28–29), Sebastian Quigley (10–11, 12–13, 16–17)